The Call to
HOLINESS

The Call to HOLINESS

Pursuing the Heart of God for the Love of the World

TIMOTHY C. TENNENT

Scripture quotations are taken from THE HOLY BIBLE, NEW INTERNATIONAL VERSION®,
NIV® Copyright © 1973, 1978, 1984, 2011 by Biblica, Inc.™ Used by permission. All rights
reserved worldwide.

Printed in the United States of America

Hardcover ISBN: 978-1-62824-163-1
Paperback ISBN: 978-1-62824-164-8
Mobi ISBN: 978-1-62824-165-5
ePub ISBN: 978-1-62824-166-2
uPDF ISBN: 978-1-62824-167-9

Library of Congress Control Number: 2014951043

Cover design by Brushfire Design Studio
Page design by PerfecType

SEEDBED PUBLISHING
Franklin, Tennessee
Seedbed.com
SOWING FOR A GREAT AWAKENING

To Bill and Carol Latimer,
for all the ways they have demonstrated
the love and holiness of Christ
in the extension of the ministry
of Asbury Theological Seminary

Contents

The Call to
HOLINESS

ONE

Holiness and the Attributes of God

Introduction

This little book is a series of reflections on the doctrine of holiness. Holiness is central to the Christian understanding of the gospel because the gospel does not begin with us or with our response to God. It begins with God Himself, who has revealed Himself as a holy God. One of the most repeated phrases in the Old Testament describing the nature of God is His statement, "I am holy." The same declaration is found in the New Testament: "But just as he who called you is holy, so be holy in all you do; for it is written: 'Be holy, because I am holy'" (1 Peter 1:15–16). We are called to be holy because He is holy. To be in relationship with God is to be brought into the household of holiness. The word *holiness* comes from

3

a Hebrew word, *kadash*, which means "to separate" or "to set apart" or "to distinguish." It is, therefore, a word about God's position in relation to us and to a world that occupies the household of sin. However, before we can even begin to explore the biblical doctrine of holiness, we must first understand the nature of all of God's attributes, and how our contemporary perspective on holiness has become distorted.

The Nature of God

If you were asked to write down a list of the attributes of God, what would that list look like? If you are like most people, you would write down such adjectives as *almighty, powerful, loving, full of grace, merciful, all-knowing, righteous, sovereign,* and titles such as *Creator, Judge, Lord, King, Heavenly Father,* and so forth. If you had time to really think about it, you might include attributes such as *omnipresent* (present everywhere), *eternal, infinite,* and so forth. You might also include the word *holy* on the list. If we spent enough time and thought on the list, I am sure that it could get very long, indeed. We might eventually begin to include things like *self-existent, uncreated, immutable* (unchangeable), and *immanent* (present with us right now).

Even if we have never taken time to sit down and make such a list, we all have some sort of list in our minds, don't we? We have a certain inner sense about what God must be like and certain actions that we are quite sure God should do or, perhaps, would never do.

I want to devote this first meditation to the two main problems we have in thinking about such a list, whether we have written it down or not. Then, I want to propose an alternative approach that avoids the two problems. Let us examine these two problems briefly.

Our Experience with Attributes

First, whatever attributes we have ascribed to God, we should realize that we have only experienced these attributes in fragmentary and imperfect ways. In other words, we have only a vague human idea of what mercy or love or holiness is, but we have never really experienced any of these attributes in their perfect form. For example, if someone says, "God is our heavenly Father," we might naturally think about our own fathers, and this might make some wonder if this really is a good description, especially if our fathers were aloof or uncaring. If we have only known corruption in human judges, then it can really influence how we might think about God as Judge. Other attributes, like omnipresence or self-existence, can become almost like theoretical ideas since we have never experienced anyone who is present everywhere, or who is not created. So, right at the threshold we are already in difficulty if we think about God's attributes only in terms of our own experience of them. What we can only know partially or, perhaps, only theoretically, God embodies in full perfection.

Putting God's Attributes in a Hierarchy

The second problem we have in thinking about God's attributes is that we tend to place them in a kind of hierarchy. In other words, we tend to see some attributes as trumping others. We think some attributes are better than others. It is not unusual, for example, to hear someone say that the God of the Old Testament is a God of judgment, whereas the God of the New Testament is a God of mercy. Statements like this are often used to imply that grace is a more important attribute or a more God-like attribute than judgment. In the Old Testament God says, "I am holy" whereas in the New Testament, the apostle John says, "God is love." Therefore, we reason, God's love must be greater than God's holiness. We end up actually pitting some of God's attributes against others and leveraging one against the other. However, the idea of ranking God's attributes, or leveraging God's love against His holiness, gets us into a lot of difficulties. We need to lay that approach aside and think about this in a different way. We cannot recover a proper understanding of holiness unless we come to see it within the proper setting of *all* of God's attributes.

A Different Way of Thinking about God's Attributes

If we go back to our list of God's attributes, it is obvious that some of them are clearly only reflected in us in tiny, fragmentary ways. Take, for example, God's eternality. We really don't know what that means from a human experience. We might think of someone who has lived a really long life, perhaps one hundred years or more. We might think about a majestic mountain that has towered over human civilization for thousands of years, but we realize that we really have no proper human reference point for thinking about eternity. We actually should have this perspective on all attributes of God. There is simply no human starting point to really grasp the full idea of any of God's attributes, even attributes like mercy, grace, or forgiveness. This is also true of the word *holiness*.

A good way to begin thinking about God's attributes properly is to temporarily suspend all our ideas about the fragmentary ways we perceive God's attributes. In their place, we must begin by making several adjustments.

First, we must recognize that all of God's attributes are always found in their full perfection. In other words, God embodies mercy perfectly. God is the perfect Judge. God is the perfect Creator. God embodies love with perfection. He alone embodies every attribute in its full perfection, and there is no attribute that finds full perfection in the human experience. (We will come back to this idea later when we look how John Wesley described holiness as being made "perfect in love.")

Second, we must cease looking at some attributes of God in isolation from His other attributes. Our natural, default way of looking at God and His attributes is to envision a great flower with many petals. God is at the center, and His petals are His attributes. We might think of grace as one petal, love as another, holiness as another, righteousness as yet another, and so forth. We must delete this image from our thinking. God's attributes are all *united* in His person, and each is informed fully and completely by His other attributes. In other words, God's love is a holy love. God's righteous judgment is fully and completely informed by His mercy. God's transcendence (His otherness) is fully informed by His immanence (His closeness). Each attribute is fully informed and shaped by the others because, in the end, God has no attributes that are separate extensions of Himself the way a flower has separate petals. Rather, God is a unified, integrated whole who, in His own nature and person, fully embodies all the attributes simultaneously in their full perfection.

With these two simple adjustments, we will make enormous progress in how we talk about God. For example, it is not unusual to hear conversations where the love of God is discussed as if it were some kind of vague emotion that describes God's feelings toward us, or where it is used as leverage against other attributes of God, particularly His holiness or His actions as righteous Judge. However, the Scriptures present God's love as a covenantal commitment to defend righteousness and to defeat and silence all rebellion. It is impossible, for example, for God to love the poor without also acting in judgment against those who oppress them. God's love and His judgment both are extended in their full perfection, and both emerge from God's own integrated being, wherein all attributes exist simultaneously. God is not merciful to the oppressed by invoking an emotive feeling about the oppressed, but rather, by overthrowing the oppressor and setting things right. The mercy and judgment of God are unified in God's nature, and both are in full perfection in the character of God. It is only when we separate attributes from one another and impose hierarchies of attributes that we fall into various errors.

A whole range of faulty thinking rampant in the church today would be swept away if even this most basic understanding of God's attributes would be understood. For example, how many times have you heard someone say in response to a comment about God's judgment or His opposition to sin, "Well, *my* God is a God of love." This represents a misunderstanding of God's attributes and not only demonstrates an isolation of one attribute from another, but puts an unwarranted wedge between one of God's attributes, holiness, and another, His love. This same problem is found when someone pits the Old Testament against the New Testament, as if two different Gods are revealed in the two testaments. This type of person demonstrates a profound misunderstanding of God's love and grace in the

Old Testament, as well as God's judgment and holiness in the New Testament. The incarnation of Jesus Christ and His death on the cross should not be seen as the trumping of God's holiness with His love, but the fullest, most perfect manifestation of both.

Conclusion

These meditations will seek to explore how God's holiness is manifested within the larger framework of His self-revelation as found in the Bible and in our lives. I hope to show that holiness is not simply a doctrine we believe in, but that it is fundamental to our relationship with God and the world. Holiness is tied to the very nature of the missional heart of God. We will see that holiness—along with all of God's other amazing attributes—always informs who He is in all of His dealings with us. In fact, a study of any of the attributes of God leads naturally to the whole character and nature of God since they are all found in an integrated whole in His person. It is my prayer that these reflections on holiness will lead us to a deeper relationship with God and one another, and will affect how we live in the world.

TWO

God's Holy Revelation of Himself

The Bible and the Holiness of God

To understand how God's holiness is revealed to us, we should first understand something about the nature of the Bible itself. The Bible is the record of God's disclosure of Himself and His saving purposes in the world. It should not be viewed primarily as a rule book on how we are to live our daily lives, even though we find plenty of guidance there. The Bible is much deeper than merely a revelation of *things we need to know*. The purpose of the Bible is not merely to help us understand *things* about God, but to help us know *Him* and His saving purposes for us. The Bible is even more than a handbook or field guide to show us how to get saved, though it is never less than that. The Bible is, at its deepest

who?
why

11

level, God's revelation of Himself. As Christians, we believe that the Bible is without error in all that it affirms. We also believe that when we read the Bible, we read it in the presence of the risen Christ and through the power of the Holy Spirit. Therefore, we read the Bible in community—with those who have read it or heard it for centuries before we ever lived, and in the ongoing presence and power of the triune God. The Scriptures reveal who God is and where we stand in relation to Him. They reveal God's saving purpose for us. The Bible is God's Word to us and to all people. It is a revelation of how we can enter into the full fellowship, beauty, abundant life, and eternal joy of the triune God.

The Bible, therefore, should be viewed more like a grand, multi-act drama or play in which God reveals truths about Himself and about us. The Scriptures record God's personal acts of redemption whereby He provides a way for us to move from our alienation from Him to full reconciliation with Him and to participate in the flourishing that is found only in His divine life. This chapter will explore the source of our alienation from God that has shattered his image in us and separated us from being full participants and partakers of His holy love.

Holiness and the Image of God

The Bible begins by revealing the majesty of God in creating the world. Because God is a perfect Creator, the creation fully reflected His perfections. This is particularly seen in His creation of men and women in His own image. As God's image-bearers, we were created to enjoy full fellowship with Him and to participate in His holiness and love. What does it mean to say that we are created in the image of God? Let me say, to begin with, that it does not refer to any physical resemblance with God because, God, in his essence, is spirit (John 4:24). The image of God refers to a deeper reality, although our physical bodies are the perfect design to manifest the image of God. While our physical bodies are an important part of how the image of God is expressed, the image of God primarily points to three realities.

What It Means to Be Created in the Image of God

First, being created in God's image means that we are endowed with a moral responsibility. We are able to bear and to obey God's commands, and we are morally accountable for our actions. Second, we are created to be in relationship with God. This means that we have the capacity to know God and to communicate with Him and therefore to be in fellowship with Him. Third, it also means that we are the extension of God's dominion and rule in the earth; we represent God. We are called to be His regents, His stewards, who represent Him before the rest of creation. So, when the Bible says that we are created in God's image, it refers to a *moral* capacity, a *relational* capacity, and a *representative* capacity.

13

These capacities are not given to the animals, at least not in the way they are granted to humans. Adam and Eve, therefore, were the bearers of God's image and were perfectly endowed with God's holiness.

Fallen in Sin

The Scriptures teach us that God created man and woman in His own image and He placed them in the Garden of Eden. They were meant to reflect His attributes and extend His glory into the world. Yet, we find an unusual thing in the Garden of Eden, which sometimes surprises first-time readers of the Bible. There is a tree, known as the Tree of Knowledge of Good and Evil, that Adam was commanded not to eat from. Why would God allow the Tree of Knowledge of Good and Evil to be present in the Garden of Eden? Wouldn't the world be "more perfect" if sin were not even possible? Why did God command Adam and Eve to "not eat from the tree of the knowledge of good and evil, for when you eat from it you will certainly die" (Gen. 2:17)? This is a mystery that we do not fully understand. However, as pointed out in the last meditation, God only acts in perfections, so we trust that this was part of God's perfect plan. One answer is that the presence of this tree is merely an acknowledgment that sin and evil had already entered the world through an earlier rebellion in God's angelic order. God may be simply acknowledging that the earlier rebellion is present and would try to spread the rebellion to the new race of humans.

But this begs the deeper question: Would the human creation have been better if we'd been created in a way that would have made it impossible for us to sin or to rebel against God? From one perspective, it would seem to ensure at the outset a holy world where only God's will would be done. It sounds like a perfect world! But upon deeper reflection, would we not be like a gigantic race of robots that simply did whatever God wanted us to do? Certainly God could have made us to serve Him in every way, but would we *love* Him? This is where the mystery of God's holiness and love (both in their full, integrated perfections) already begins to be seen. True love involves choices. An all-powerful ruler can make someone obey, but he can't make someone love. Aren't human will and free choice integral to the manifestation of love? Apparently God receives His greatest glory, not merely from acts of obedience, but through our *choosing* to participate with Him through our free response to His initiatives of grace. Although it is a mystery we may never fully understand, it seems that the possibility of rejection had to be present in order for the possibility of love to become part of our relationship with God.

The Relationship between Free Will and Love

Choices are important and vital if we are to have a doctrine of positive holiness, not just innocence. In other words, holiness must be confirmed by real choices that we make that draw us into a full relationship with God. A machine can work flawlessly, but it cannot ever be holy, because that involves capacities that machines do not have. You cannot have a relationship with a machine. As much as you may love your computer, your talking GPS, or your iPhone, there are real limits to your capacity to relate to a machine! Choice is integrally related to love, which is why love operates at the highest level of relationships.

In the Garden of Eden, Adam and Eve were created in holiness, but that holiness would not rise above mere positive innocence if there were no possibility of it being confirmed through a positive act of obedience that drew them through their own volition into the full circle of the divine life. But, this also meant that the possibility of rejection was there. We can choose to go our own way and live our lives separated from God. God is not the author of evil. However, He allowed the possibility of human choices for the greater possibility of a real relationship with Him. This means that the story of God's work with the human race is long and arduous. It would ultimately involve the Father sending His Son into the world to die, and the sending of His Spirit to indwell us. All of this is integrally related to what is necessary for us to know Him in His fullness.

In the Garden the first humans were offered a choice to obey or disobey God. The fruit of the Tree of Knowledge of Good and Evil was like a sacrament in reverse—an anti-sacrament. Rather than a means of grace to know God, as we see in the later Christian sacrament of communion, this was like a means of rebellion that allured us into joining the rebellion against God. Precisely because God said, "Do not eat of that fruit," it became the focal point of a possible rebellion against God. We often define a *sacrament* as an outward and visible sign of an inward and spiritual grace. However, in the Garden we meet an *anti-sacrament*, which is an outward and visible sign of an inward and spiritual rebellion. So Satan offered Eve the anti-sacrament. Eve ate and she gave some to Adam, and he ate—both entering into the fellowship and communion of the rebellion.

Sin entered the human race, thereby shattering the full expression of the image of God in men and women. It is like a virus on a computer system that spreads to the entire network. In eating the fruit, Adam was not just acting on his own, but acting as a representative man. He acted on behalf of the whole human race. When Adam ate, we were all brought into this rebellion. A physical and spiritual inertia of death was unleashed. This was the breaking of a relationship with God, thereby separating us from God's holiness.

At the dawn of creation, Satan achieved an important victory over the human race. It was one that would cause great pain and suffering and lead many to eternal death. But, thanks be to God, the Lord God Almighty always has

17

the last word! What happened because of that first act of disobedience in the first garden, Eden, would someday be reversed through an act of obedience in the second garden, the Garden of Gethsemane. However, other stories must be told to prepare us for this. We must pause at this point and recognize that God is holy and we are not. We are outside of His fellowship, and we live in brokenness. The fall is, at its root, a shattering and marring of our relationship with God and thereby, our capacity to reflect the holiness of God. The work of redemption is the restoration of that relationship, and ultimately, the reconstitution of holiness in our lives.

gospel!
reconciliation
healing the brokenness

THREE

God Calls His People to Be Holy

One of the questions people often ask is, why did God choose the Jewish people? There are thousands of people groups in the world, so why did God choose the Jews? Perhaps you remember William Ewer's famous quip: "How odd of God to choose the Jews." He could have chosen the Egyptians or the Hittites or the Incas. The Scriptures say that God did not choose Israel because they were more numerous or more powerful than any other nation, but simply because He wanted to show them His love (Deut. 7:7–8). Sometimes people mistakenly think that by choosing Israel, God was excluding other nations and showing them some kind of favoritism compared to other peoples. However, from the beginning, when God first called Abraham and made a covenant with Israel, He made it clear that He was blessing the descendants of Abraham (Israel) <u>*so that*</u> they might be a blessing to every nation on earth. Genesis 12 records the covenant God made with Abraham. He said, "I will make you into a great nation, and I will bless you; I will make your name great, and you will be a blessing. I will bless those who bless you, and whoever curses you I will curse; *and all peoples on earth will be blessed through you*" (vv. 2–3, emphasis added).

God chose Israel as the instrument through which He would restore His image to humanity and bring blessing to the whole world. When God later repeated the covenant to Abraham, He said that it was through his seed that all nations would be blessed (Gen. 22:18). That seed was an early hint that God would send to earth His only Son, Jesus, who was the seed, or offspring, of the Jewish nation. In the New Testament, the apostle Paul made this clear when he said, "Scripture does not say 'and to seeds,' meaning many people, but 'and to your seed,' meaning one person, who is Christ" (Gal. 3:16).

From the outset God had a plan to send His Son into the world to reestablish His presence in the world. Sin is, at its root, the absence of God. Holiness, at its root, is the presence of God. There would be no greater invasion of God's holiness in the world than that of sending His Son, Jesus Christ, into the world. He would, therefore, establish a single people, Israel, and call them to holiness in order to demonstrate before the world what it meant to be a people brought back into relationship with Him. This was to prepare the world for the coming of Christ. Israel was also to prepare the world for the day when we would be called to "disciple the nations" and thereby reestablish God's holiness in every nation of the world. But the first step in this grand drama would be to start with one nation and reveal God's holiness to them.

God's Covenant with Abraham

God's covenant with Abraham, found in Genesis (12:1–3; 17:5–6; 18:18–19; 22:17–18), contains three distinct parts. First, God would bless Abraham numerically by giving him many descendants. Second, He would give the Israelites a land (this is why it is called the 'promised land'). Third, He would use them to bless all nations on earth. The word *nations* here does not mean political countries as we know them today, but each and every ethnic group in the world, which number in the thousands.

The descendants of Abraham did multiply and eventually relocated to Egypt, where they were enslaved for four hundred years by Egyptian pharaohs. At the right time, God appeared to Moses in a burning bush and told him that he was on holy ground. The presence of God was holy, and Moses was being called to lead the Israelites into a new level of their relationship with God. They were led out of Egypt and were given the Law.

The Law of God

The Law was nothing more than a covenant between God and the Israelites that would establish them as a holy people. They were given 613 distinctive laws that would set them apart from the nations. Some of the commands make perfect sense to us, such as "Do not deceive your neighbor" or "Do not hold back the wages of a hired man overnight" or "Do not curse the deaf or put a stumbling block in front of the blind." Other commands seem very strange to us, such as "Do not plant your field with two kinds of seed" (Lev. 19:19) or "Do not wear clothes of wool and linen woven together" (Deut. 22:11). Before we dismiss these strange commands out of hand, as sometimes happens today, we should remember several important things.

The Purpose of the Law

First, the purpose of the Law was to create and form a people who were distinctive and separate (holy) from the surrounding nations. It was common among the Canaanites (a neighboring nation) to practice what was known as "sympathetic magic." This is the idea of, in the case of seed, "marrying" two kinds of seed in order to produce "offspring." It was a cultic idea that, at its core, denied that God is the source of all life and fruitfulness. Therefore, commands that may seem strange to us were actually deeply contextual commands that were specific to Israel in order to establish them as holy.

22

Their Covenant Is Not Our Covenant

Second, as Christians we must remember that we are under a different covenant than the Jews were under. All of the Bible is God's Word *for* us, but it is not all God's word *to* us. The old covenant, or Old Testament, was *their* covenant; it is not *our* covenant. All of Scripture is fully inspired and wholly profitable for teaching us about God, but not all of it is God's direct command to we who are now under a different covenant.

Let me use an analogy to help us understand the relationship between the two covenants. If someone works for General Motors, he or she is under a contract that lays out the stipulations of employment, the obligations of the employer, and the privileges and responsibilities of the employed, as long as that person works for General Motors. However, when a new contract is offered, the old contract is null and void, and the workers are put under the new contract. We all understand this. If you compare the two contracts, there will, of course, be many things that are true of both contracts. There are certain obligations that are carried forward into the new contract, but they are only binding on an employee if the new stipulations are explicitly brought forward into the new contract. This is an imprecise analogy, but I hope it will help you understand the main point. This is why the writer of Hebrews said, "By calling this covenant 'new,' he has made the first one obsolete" (Heb. 8:13). In some cases, there are Old Testament laws that are not carried over (like planting your field with two kinds of seed). In other cases, there are commands that are brought directly over, such as the command to not steal (compare Exodus 20:15 with Mark 10:19, Romans 2:21, and Ephesians 4:28). The point is that there are many commands in the Old Testament that we are also called to obey because they are found in our covenant as well. It is common today to hear people undercut the commands of Scripture in the New Testament by citing commands that are no longer binding on us today from the Old Testament. This demonstrates a profound misunderstanding of the nature of the two covenants.

Is the Old Testament Way "Hard" and the New Testament Way "Easy"?

It is sometimes falsely believed that the Old Testament is filled with harsh commands and that things are much easier under the New Testament, or new covenant. However, some of the older commands are actually deepened from outward acts to the inward intentions of the heart. For example, the Old Testament called the people of God to love their neighbors. Jesus calls us to also love our enemies (Matt. 5:44). The Old Testament forbade God's people from committing adultery (Ex. 20:14). That command is carried over to Luke 18:20, but we are told, in addition, that it is sinful to

24

even look at a woman with lust in our hearts (Matt. 5:28). The reason Jesus says that his "yoke is easy and [his] burden is light" (Matt. 11:30) is not because the demands of the New Testament are less than those in the Old. Rather, it is because under the new covenant we now live out the even deeper moral demands of God in the presence of the risen Christ and through the power of the Holy Spirit. There is a line from a poem by John Bunyan that beautifully captures this:

> To run and to walk the Law demands,
> But gives us neither feet nor hands;
> Better news the gospel brings,
> It bids us fly *and* gives us wings!

The Law as a Tutor to Lead Us to Christ

The main point here is to see that even though we are not under the authority of the old covenant, all 613 commands were specific to forming Israel as a separate, holy nation. To say that God could never have given these commands, either because we do not understand the commands or because they are not renewed in our covenant, is to pit the God of the Old Testament against the God of the New Testament. This is an old heresy that was most notably taught by an early Christian known as Marcion, who lived in the second century. He taught that the God of the Old Testament was a vengeful, wrathful God who was a separate and lower being from the God of the New Testament, who is all-forgiving and full of grace. The church rightly rejected this view as heresy. Interestingly, it was declared a heresy because the view failed to see the mercy and grace of God in the Old Testament, and because Marcion ignored major passages in the New Testament that reveal the wrath and judgment of God. It is important to see that the whole Bible reveals to us the full nature of God. It is wrong to pit one verse against another. Instead, we should see it as a multifaceted diamond with many dimensions, and only by seeing all of it together is the full beauty and glory revealed.

The Law may seem harsh to us at times, but God knew it was the necessary tutor to teach us what we needed to know about His opposition to sin, and the necessary measures that were required to forge a people separated unto Himself in holiness. Our tendency to misunderstand many things in the Old Testament is because, as noted in the first chapter, we tend to pluck out certain attributes of God in isolation from others and use them in unwarranted ways, rather than to hold them all together so we might get a full picture of who God is. Even though we are no longer under the Law, Paul says that the Law is good and holy (Rom. 7:12). It was not sufficient to save us, but it was crucial for pointing us to the pathway of holiness that would lead us to Christ (Gal. 3:24–25).

FOUR

God's Judgment and Holiness

In the last chapter we learned that the purpose of the Law was to create a holy people. This is far more than people merely doing good things. It is ultimately about the full manifestation of God's presence with His people. This is why the essence of sin is choosing the absence of God. In contrast, holiness, at its very foundation, is the sign and seal of God's presence in the world. However, we misunderstand the full scope of God's presence in the world if we do not have a proper understanding of the judgment of God. Indeed, these meditations on holiness are rebuilding several areas in the church's witness that have been lost in the contemporary period. One of the most glaring examples has been the loss of a proper understanding of the judgment of God. This misunderstanding, in turn, has led to problems in a proper doctrine of holiness. Because God's holiness is the basis for all of God's judgments, and because, for many in the modern world, this seems to be in conflict with their understanding of God's grace, forgiveness, and mercy, we will need to explore what the Scripture teaches about God's judgment and clarify a number of things that are widely misunderstood today.

When God judges the world, He does so by holding up His standard of righteousness. Because God is perfectly righteous, He does not, as we often do, grade on a curve. In other words, God does not measure us to determine if we are mostly righteous or mostly wicked and make up the difference with a dose of grace. This is, once again, a misunderstanding of the attributes of God that pits them against one another or holds them in some kind of unwarranted tension. It is not even true to say that the attributes of God balance one another out. That is to impose a human understanding on God.

When the Scripture declares that God is righteous, it means that He is perfectly righteous, or infinitely righteous. This means that even the smallest sin cannot go unchallenged in the presence of God. In fact, the New Testament teaches that "whoever keeps the whole law and yet stumbles at just one point is guilty of breaking all of it" (James 2:10). Why does the New Testament teach this? It seems so contrary to our way of thinking. James explains the reason in the next verse, "For he who said, 'You shall not commit adultery,' also said, 'You shall not murder.'" The point is that when we disobey God's commandments, it is not merely a rejection of a particular point in the legal code. Rather, it is to stand against God Himself. It is to oppose His righteous rule and reign in our lives and in the world. The New Testament understands sin as opposing God and rebelling against who He is, not merely as breaking rules and regulations. This is fundamental to our understanding of holiness. Holiness is not merely about keeping laws or rules better than the next person. Holiness is about our whole relationship with God, and how we embody His image personally and before the world.

The judgment of God is called forth whenever God holds up His infinite standard of righteousness and holiness against the world. Sin must be judged. Romans teaches that "the wages of sin is death" (Rom. 6:23). To put it another way, God looks at the world and sees all of the destructive powers of evil unleashed in the world, and He is determined to set it right and restore His creation to its original design of glory and holiness. The Scriptures are filled with examples of God's judgment being extended into the world.

Some Representative Examples of Judgment in the Bible

Sometimes we read examples of God's judgment in the Bible that are quite stunning. Let me list a few:

1. The sons of Aaron, Nadab and Abihu, were consumed by fire from God's presence because they brought unauthorized fire into the Holy of Holies (Lev. 10:1–3).

2. A man was stoned to death for collecting wood on the Sabbath day (Num. 15:32–36).

3. Those who joined Korah in his rebellion against Moses were swallowed alive by the earth (Num. 16:31–34).

4. Ananias and Sapphira were struck dead by God for conspiring together to lie about the gift of their property to the church (Acts 5:1–11).

5. Herod was struck down by God for not giving Him the glory (Acts 12:20–23).

6. A man in the church was caught having sexual intercourse with his father's wife. The apostle Paul turned the man "over to Satan for the destruction of the flesh, so that his spirit may be saved" (1 Cor. 5:1–5).

7. On the final Judgment Day, anyone whose name is not found in the Book of Life is thrown into a lake of fire (Rev. 20:11–15).

8. We must all appear before the judgment seat of Christ (2 Cor. 5:10)

I could cite many more examples, but I have chosen a few of the most memorable so that we can face the challenge of texts like these head-on. We will examine these texts under three themes: first, the rightness of God's judgment; second, the timing of God's judgment; and finally, the proportionality of God's judgment.

The Rightness of God's Judgment

God's authority and right to judge us is rooted in the doctrine of creation. The Scriptures teach that God is the Creator of the world: "The earth is the LORD's, and everything in it, the world, and all who live in it" (Ps. 24:1). Since He created us, we belong to Him and are accountable to Him. We are not autonomous without any accountability. A strong doctrine of creation has been eroding in Christian circles for the last few decades. We already established in chapter 2 that central to our understanding of the image of God is that we have been given moral capacities. Positively, this grants us remarkable capacities for righteous, sacrificial work in the world. But it also means that we are held accountable to God, and that He exercises the right to judge us. The Scriptures teach that "the wages of sin is death" (Rom. 6:23). Therefore, because all of us have sinned, we are worthy of God's judgment and we live only because of the extension of His grace and mercy. The list cited earlier notes three examples from the Old Testament and five from the New Testament to clarify that this is a consistent teaching throughout the Scriptures. God's righteous judgment is taught in both of the ancient ecumenical creeds (the Apostles' Creed and the Nicene Creed) of the church.

Indeed, there are hundreds of verses in the Bible to support this doctrine. Furthermore, the psalms regularly assert that it is a matter of great joy that God will judge the world and its people, for that will finally set all things right.

The Timing of God's Judgment

The world's jeering doubts about the final judgment of God are as old as Noah. However, a more recent development is that leaders in the church are now claiming that certain judgments recorded in the Bible are inconsistent with what we know of the nature of God. The texts they cite are normally examples of God's immediate acts of judgment in history. A quick look at the list of examples given earlier will demonstrate that some of the judgments of God are immediate and some are delayed. For example, some acts of judgment immediately followed the disobedience, such as the man caught collecting wood on the Sabbath day, or Nadab and Abihu after they offered unauthorized fire before the Lord, or Herod at the very moment he received praise that he was like God. Other judgments, such as the ones recorded in Revelation 20 or 2 Corinthians 5:10, occur after the end of all human history, and therefore represent a delay until after we have died.

In this contemporary period it is becoming common to hear even pastors objecting to immediate acts of God's judgment. However, the Scriptures teach that God purposely judges some immediately, and at other times He chooses to delay His righteous judgment until the end. Why is this? This is because bringing some judgments forward to the present and delaying other judgments to the end serves God's purposes. By bringing some judgments forward, He is able to demonstrate in a vivid way the consequences of sin that may not be taken seriously if we never saw the result of rebellion against God. When Paul looked back on the Old Testament, he recalled not only God's great redemptive acts, like bringing Israel through the Red Sea on dry ground, but also God's judgments against Israel. He even cited in particular the time when twenty-three thousand people died because of Israelites who had engaged in sexual immorality with the daughters of Moab (see 1 Corinthians 10:8; Numbers 25). Yet, Paul looked back on it all and said, "These things occurred as examples to keep us from setting our hearts on evil things as they did" (1 Cor. 10:6). He then listed other examples of God's judgments and, again, he said, "These things happened to them as examples and were written down as warnings for us (1 Cor. 10:11). The New Testament clearly does not seek to distance itself from the examples of the immediate judgment of God found in the Old Testament. On the contrary, it teaches that these have been recorded for our own warning and instruction. They are actually a means of grace for us, not an embarrassment that we need to somehow explain away.

Just as immediate judgment quickens our hearts and leads us to repentance, delayed judgment gives the necessary time for reflection, repentance, and the reception of the means of grace. Thus, both timings of judgment serve God's purposes. We do not know why God judges some things immediately and why others are delayed. But we do know (from chapter 1) that God is the perfect Judge, and therefore the ratio between judgment now and judgment delayed is perfectly calibrated for the maximum benefit of God's glory and our holiness. The two expressions of God's judgment are perfect in wisdom, since the judgment and holiness of God are only found in their full perfection.

The Proportionality of God's Judgment

Finally, it is important to regain a biblical perspective on the proportionality of the judgments we find in the Scriptures. In the Old Testament, God gave the command that the Israelites were to keep the Sabbath day holy. In order to keep it holy, they were instructed not to perform any work on that day. The first person to disobey this command (a man caught collecting firewood on the Sabbath) was brought before the Lord and it was confirmed that he should be stoned to death. For some modern readers this is a judgment out of proportion to the crime. However, it is important to remember that this judgment was not merely about a particular law being broken. It was a deeper sign of the man's rebellion against

34

the righteous rule and reign of God. In the Scriptures, rebelling against God's rule and reign is a capital offense. In the end, all those who rebel against God's rule and reign in the world will be judged. Holiness is about our response to God Himself, not just about keeping a legal code. Most of the examples of these immediate acts of judgment follow key moments in the life of God's people: the giving of the Law, the birth of the church at Pentecost, and so forth. Therefore, these judgments are clear warnings for us to take who God is and what He is doing in the world seriously.

Conclusion

In today's climate, there is a strong desire to emphasize the verses in the Bible on God's grace, mercy, and forgiveness and to downplay or ignore any passages related to God's judgment and holiness. However, we must realize that to lose any of God's attributes is to lose the full knowledge of God that, in turn, only further fractures His image in us. As we will see, it also diminishes the magnitude of what Christ took upon Himself on the cross.

FIVE

The Cross as the Great Transaction of Holiness

The cross of Jesus Christ is God's answer to the greatest human predicament in history. Quite plainly, the predicament is that every single human since Adam has not only been born into sin through the original fall, but has confirmed Adam's rebellion by his or her own rebellion against God. The Bible declares, "There is no one righteous, not even one" (see Psalms 14:1–3, Romans 3:10–12). Therefore, the whole human race is born into sin, bound by sin, and, under God's righteous judgment, deserving of death. This is the conundrum: How can the human race be rescued out of rebellion and avoid the inevitable condemnation when, without exception, everyone is inescapably a part of it? Who can deliver the human race?

Since Adam's rebellion brought sin into the whole human race (see Romans 5:12), we are in an impossible situation. No human deliverer is eligible to save the human race, since all have sinned. But what if a second Adam could be brought into the world? What if you could actually re-create the original situation, where Adam was placed in the Garden, given a choice to obey or disobey, but this time get it right? It would be like stopping the human race, pushing the rewind button, going back to the beginning, and getting to redo the first tragic scene that we call "the fall."

Why it's called Good News

In the gospel, we come to understand that God undertakes a radical, universe-shaking solution. Since the entire human race is ineligible to bring the redemptive rescue, God knew that the only solution was if He Himself became a man and entered the human race as a New Adam (or a second Adam). In the most amazing act of condescension and mercy, God became a man, but one untainted by all human sin. Christ, the eternal Son of God, was thereby born into the human race as a second Adam. Satan tried, as he did the first Adam, to tempt Jesus and to bring him into the rebellion. Jesus spent forty days in the wilderness after His baptism, being tempted by the evil one. This was a relentless period of an all-out assault on Jesus by the forces of the rebellion. But unlike Adam, Jesus chose to obey God. He never sinned. He had the capacity as the God-man to either sin or not sin, because although Jesus was one person, He had two natures:

a divine nature and a human nature. He had a will. As the second Adam, He could have chosen to disobey God. Yet, Jesus chose to obey God fully and completely.

The result of the incarnation of God in Jesus Christ is that we now have two Adams. We have two heads of two different races: the first Adam, who is the head of a race under condemnation; and a second Adam, who is the Head of a new, redeemed humanity. If we trust in Christ, then we become a part of His obedience in the same way that we had formerly been a part of the first Adam's rebellion. First Corinthians 15:45 says, "The first man Adam became a living being; the last Adam, a life-giving spirit."

The Cross: a Satisfaction of God's Holiness and the Transference of Alien Holiness to Us

Christ alone lived a holy life without sin. Therefore, Jesus' death was offered up as a substitution for us. Jesus bore the penalty of our sins upon the cross of Calvary. The cross is an astonishing expression of God's grace and mercy as well as God's holiness and justice, all expressed simultaneously in their full perfection. God's holiness and justice require that sins be paid for in full. Sin cannot be ignored or swept under the rug. Satisfaction must be made. God's righteous judgment was poured on Jesus Christ, who bore the sins of the world. Yet, that very act of judgment was also the greatest expression of God's love for us. It was God's grace and mercy

His choice — not forced. Not too excited about it but willing to submit to God

Call To Holiness

that sent His only Son as a substitution for us. He paid the debt that we owed. The Scriptures teach us that Jesus bore our sins on the cross. We often think of the cross only through the lens of being cleansed from sin, but the cross is not only the satisfaction of our guilt, fear, and shame. It is the transference of His holiness to us. In other words, through the cross we not only lose our sins, but we gain His righteousness.

This is, of course, an alien righteousness. This means that it is a righteousness that comes as God's gift to us. We have not earned it. As we will see later, God is not satisfied that we have only an alien righteousness. Nevertheless, this is the beginning of holiness. We must understand that holiness begins at the cross of Jesus Christ. Holiness begins by realizing our own incapacity to be holy. Holiness begins by realizing that the source of all holiness is in Jesus.

The Cross as a Delay of God's Judgment and the Time of God's Favor

The incarnation, life, death, and resurrection of Jesus Christ represent a dramatic move by God to bring good news to a lost world. This is the time of God's favor. This means that God is delaying much of His righteous judgment so that as many people as possible may hear the gospel. Because we are currently in a period of largely delayed judgment, this has given the impression to some that either judgment belongs to the Old Testament or that judgment is not really an

40

appropriate action of God. However, as we demonstrated in the last chapter, both of these assumptions are false. We have already seen that some immediate judgment of God does take place in the New Testament, and we know from church history that God continues to judge people and nations. It is also wrong-headed to say that judgment is not appropriate for God now that we live on this side of the cross. On the contrary, the cross of Jesus Christ is the place where God's judgment is poured out. Furthermore, those who refuse to accept God's news in Jesus Christ must still face the judgment of God. This is clearly taught in Scripture. In 2 Thessalonians the apostle Paul spoke of God's judgment that will come at the return of Christ:

> All this is evidence that God's judgment is right, and as a result you will be counted worthy of the kingdom of God, for which you are suffering. God is just: He will pay back trouble to those who trouble you and give relief to you who are troubled, and to us as well. This will happen when the Lord Jesus is revealed from heaven in blazing fire with his powerful angels. He will punish those who do not know God and do not obey the gospel of our Lord Jesus. They will be punished with everlasting destruction and shut out from the presence of the Lord and from the glory of his might on the day he comes to be glorified in his holy people and to be marveled at among all those who have believed. This includes you, because you believed our testimony to you. (1:5–10)

Texts like this are rarely preached on in the contemporary church. This is why it is so important for Christians

The thing is, how God
we don't know
intends to bring it about — the shots are
we try to call the as if we are
judge.

to become daily readers of the Scriptures and to discover personally the great mysteries of the faith contained there.

We have now told the story of how God, through His Son, has reestablished holiness in the world. However, this is a righteousness that is foreign to us. It has been declared of us, but not yet wrought in us. The following chapters will show how God takes the alien righteousness of Christ and makes it a reality in our lives. We will see that this is also impossible without God's action and initiative in our lives. In fact, it will only be possible through the work of the third person of the Trinity, the Holy Spirit.

SIX

Pentecost and the Spirit of Holiness

We have now seen how trusting in Christ has made us holy, but that it is an alien righteousness. In other words, it is a righteousness that belongs to Christ, but as an act of God's grace, it is attributed to us. But to effectively serve Christ in the world, we must not merely be called holy; we must actually be holy. This is why Jesus told the apostles before His ascension to wait in Jerusalem "until you have been clothed with power from on high" (Luke 24:49). At His ascension He repeated this, saying, "You will receive power when the Holy Spirit comes on you; and you will be my witnesses in Jerusalem, and in all Judea and Samaria, and to the end of the earth" (Acts 1:8). On the Day of Pentecost, the disciples were all gathered together in an upper room. Suddenly there was a sound of wind and fire, and they were all "filled with the Holy Spirit" (Acts 2:4). This is a very important event in the unfolding of God's redemptive plan. Pentecost is the event whereby the Holy Spirit comes in full power to enable Christians who have been declared righteous to actually be righteous. It is not that the Day of Pentecost itself makes the church righteous, but this is the beginning of the full ministry of the Holy Spirit in the life of the church. This chapter will seek to unfold some of the key things that took place because of the Holy Spirit's outpouring on the Day of Pentecost and beyond.

Pentecost and the Outpouring of the Holy Spirit

First, Pentecost is the day when God clearly demonstrates that salvation and redemption are the work of the triune God. The Father is the source, the initiator, and the final goal of all the redemptive acts of God. The Son is the embodiment of the mission of God. The work of salvation is accomplished through His birth, life, death, resurrection, and ascension. The Holy Spirit is the empowering presence of God who makes us holy.

Second, the Holy Spirit now dwells among us. The Holy Spirit is God Himself acting in this world and in our lives. He draws us by His grace to the Father. He intercedes with us and within us, helping us to pray. The Holy Spirit teaches and admonishes us when we read Scripture. He gives us the gift of discernment so that we might have the mind of

Christ and think about things in ways that are informed by godly wisdom. He applies and nurtures the fruit of the Spirit in our lives (love, joy, peace, patience, goodness, kindness, gentleness, faithfulness, and self-control). The Holy Spirit assures us of our forgiveness and our adoption as the children of God. In short, the Holy Spirit mediates the presence of God in our lives and in the church.

Third, the Holy Spirit empowers the church for effective service, witness, and global mission. Jesus promised that the Holy Spirit would empower us to be His witnesses to the ends of the earth (Acts 1:8). It is the Holy Spirit who enables the church to serve sacrificially and to be an effective witness unto Christ and the gospel. Holiness, as we shall see, is not just about making us personally righteous, but it is about extending God's glory and righteousness to all peoples of the world! There are thousands of people groups who still have not received the good news about Jesus Christ. It is the Holy Spirit who makes sure that the gospel is proclaimed to the ends of the earth through the empowered witness of the church.

Fourth, the Holy Spirit is the One who continues to manifest redemptive signs of God's kingdom breaking into the world. The good news of God's powerful work in this world did not stop at the cross and resurrection of Jesus Christ. It is too small to think that we are called to simply proclaim something that happened in history thousands of years ago. While the cross and resurrection form the central proclamation of the church, we also acknowledge that the good news of God's reign continues to unfold. All the future realities of heaven (healing, forgiveness, reconciliation, deliverance from evil, and so forth) are breaking into the world now through the presence of the Holy Spirit. Men and women are healed by the power of the Holy Spirit. They experience forgiveness and reconciliation with one another. The poor and downcast receive hope. The Holy Spirit applies all the future realities of the New Creation to the present. This process will not be fully complete until Jesus returns, but if we look around, we can see that God is still at work by His Spirit, reconciling the world to Himself.

Fifth, the Holy Spirit is the One who makes us holy. The presence of the Holy Spirit, God's empowering presence in us, leads to transformational holiness in our lives, in society, and in the world. As God's empowering presence, the Holy Spirit embodies the New Creation, including purity of holiness. This should really begin to expand our understanding of the full dimensions of holiness in our lives. In chapter 4, we saw that holiness is the sign and seal of God's presence in the world. This means that we must expand our ideas regarding what it means for God's holiness to be reintroduced into the world. We mostly think of it in terms of personal holiness. We understand God's presence as eradicating sin in our lives. This is an important aspect of holiness. However, God's presence also challenges and transforms the society we live in. In other words, social holiness is also crucial to a proper understanding of biblical holiness. God's transformative work infuses not only our individual lives, but also the whole structure of culture and society. Moreover, holiness is not only personal and social; it is also missional. This means that holiness is not just about our being transformed, or even our culture reflecting certain things, but it causes us to think missionally about the world and how we can mirror God's actions in the world.

The last three chapters of this book are dedicated to exploring how holiness invades our lives personally, socially, and missionally, to the ends of the earth.

SEVEN

Holiness, Entire Sanctification, and the Redirected Heart

On May 24, 1738, John Wesley had his famous heartwarming experience at Aldersgate. Wesley went "unwillingly" down to a Christian society meeting, and there encountered a reading of Martin Luther's preface to Paul's Epistle to the Romans. Listen to Wesley's own words in describing what happened:

> About a quarter before nine, while the reader was describing the change which God works in the heart through faith in Christ, I felt my heart strangely warmed. I felt I did trust in Christ alone for salvation; and an assurance was given me that He had taken away my sins, even mine, and saved me from the law of sin and death.

Wesley, by the grace of God, heard the full force of Paul when he said, "For in the gospel the righteousness of God is revealed—a righteousness that is by faith from first to last" (Rom. 1:17). This is one of those foundational doctrines that defines Christian identity. The doctrine of justification by faith is a doctrine that everyone really needs to personally hear at some deep level. You need to believe it—but you also need to *experience* it. This is precisely what happened to Wesley on May 24, 1738. For convenience sake, let's call this the May 24 story. You need to have a May 24 story. It may not happen to you on May 24—you may not even remember the date, but you need a May 24 story. This is your stake in the ground. This is that point where you say to the Lord, "I do trust in Christ alone for my salvation, and an assurance is given to me that my sins, even mine, are taken away, and I am delivered from the law of sin and death."

There are some stories that must be told before other stories are possible. You must have a May 24 story as a prerequisite to the Holy Spirit's further work of sanctification. Both stories are the result of God's grace, but they are two different stories. Wesley had his May 24 story, but he also had an encounter with the Holy Spirit on January 1.

It was on New Year's Eve, bringing in the year 1739, that Wesley attended another society meeting. He went down, not to Aldersgate, but to Fetter Lane. That night at Fetter Lane, Wesley attended a prayer meeting that was a night watch vigil to bring in the New Year. While they were praying, at around 3:00 AM, something dramatic happened to Wesley. He received a sanctifying experience where God reoriented his heart and life. Wesley wrote in his journal:

> [On Monday morning, January 1, 1739,] Mr. Hall . . . and my brother Charles, were present at our love-feast in Fetter Lane, with about sixty of our brethren. At about three in the morning, as we were continuing instant in prayer, the power of God came mightily among us, insomuch that many cried out for exceeding joy, and many fell to the ground. As soon as we were recovered a little from that awe and amazement at the presence of His majesty, we broke out with one voice, "We praise thee, O God, we acknowledge thee to be the Lord." (*Works of John Wesley*, 3rd ed., vol. 1 (Grand Rapids: Baker Books, 2007), 170).

Wesley believed in sanctification as a doctrine before 1739, but it was here that he experienced it. It became a new chapter in his spiritual journey. Perhaps we can call this his Fetter Lane story. There is the May 24 story, and there is the Fetter Lane story—both are essential in the life of the believer. Wesley's life was reoriented. He became sanctified. He was filled with the Holy Spirit.

Entire Sanctification

The doctrine of entire sanctification is one of the most misunderstood doctrines in the Methodist movement. It is misunderstood because we haven't been prepared to hear it. When most of us hear the word *sanctification* we think of it as a legal or forensic term. In other words, we think that being "sanctified" means that you have been divinely certified before God's court of justice as someone without any sin in your life, and once sanctified, you will never sin again. That is not what Wesley taught or meant by sanctification. For Wesley, sanctification was not really a legal term at all. You could be justified alone on a deserted island, but sanctification must take place in the context of relationship. Sin is, therefore, not merely the deeds we do that break God's law; it is the expression of a broken relationship. Whenever we sin, at that moment of choosing sin, we are actually electing the absence of God in our lives at that point. You see, sanctification is always relational. Sin separates us from God. Sin is our embrace of the absence of God in our lives.

This is the great insight of the holiness movement. The holiness movement reminds us that alien righteousness is not God's last word for the believer. Salvation is about more than justification. Righteousness for Wesley was about more than God just looking at us through a different set of glasses. Alien righteousness must become native righteousness; imputed righteousness must become actualized righteousness; declared righteousness must become embodied righteousness, wrought in us not by our own strength but through the power of the living God. We are marked, oriented, and reoriented by love.

Wesley taught that we are justified by faith and we are sanctified by faith. We are justified by faith in Jesus Christ, but we are sanctified by faith as we come into full relationship with the triune God. It is not true that we are justified by God's action and we are sanctified by our actions. No, both justification and sanctification begin with God's prior action in our lives that calls for our response.

As a relational term, entire sanctification means that your whole life, your body, and your spirit have been reoriented. Entire sanctification means that your entire heart has been reoriented toward the joyful company of the triune God. Sanctification was, for Wesley, not the end of some long drudge out of the life of sin, but joining the assembly of those who have truly found joy. For Wesley, holiness was the crown of true happiness. Sanctification is what purifies us from everything that "contaminates body and spirit, perfecting holiness out of reverence for God" (2 Cor. 7:1).

Sin is encamped around us on every side, but it is no longer our ally. We leave behind the agonizingly torn hearts, where we always live under condemnation because sin is always creeping back into our desires. To be sanctified is to receive a second blessing, a gift from God. It is a gift that changes our hearts, reorients our relationship with the triune God and with others, and gives us the capacity to love God and our neighbor in new and profound ways. It transforms our whole life because our hearts have been reoriented.

Sanctified people still sin. However, the difference is that in the life of a sanctified person, sin becomes your permanent enemy and no longer your secret lover!

The language of "entire sanctification" uses the word "entire" in reference to Greek, not Latin. In Greek "entire" or "complete" can still be improved upon. H. C. Morrison, the founder of Asbury Theological Seminary, once said, "There is no state of grace that cannot be improved on." J. C. McPheeters, the second president of Asbury, was once asked, "How are you doing?" He joyfully replied, "I'm improving." Sanctification is a new orientation that no longer looks back longingly on the old life, but is always looking forward to the New Creation. It is a life that has been engulfed by new realities—eternal realities—not the realities of that which is passing away.

Wesley also understood that holiness is not merely a negative term. It is not just about sins that we avoid. If you were to eradicate every sin in your life, you would only be halfway to holiness. This is because for Wesley, holiness was never just about sins we avoid; it was about fruit we produce! In Wesley, faith and fruit meet and are joyfully wed! We no longer have a view of holiness that is legalistic, private, negative, and static. It is not merely legal, but relational; not merely private, but embedded in community; not negative, but the joyful advance of God's rule and reign. When Wesley calls us to be "made perfect in love," he is not envisioning that we are without sin. Wesley actually never used the phrase "sinless perfection." Rather, he meant that we have been oriented toward God's love, which is found in full perfection (as explained in chapter 1). Perfect love does not mean that we have climbed the ladder of works and attained perfection. Rather, it means that we have fully surrendered to the power of God's grace in our lives. We never stop growing in God's grace. It is instantaneous in the sense that it is God's gift to us that reorients our hearts. It is a lifetime process.

One of the best metaphors I ever heard for perfect love was a story told by Dr. Robert Coleman, who taught at Asbury Seminary for twenty-seven years. Dr. Coleman was out in the garden, working, on a hot day, with sweat pouring off his body. His son saw him through the window of the house and decided to bring him a glass of water. The boy went down to the kitchen, pulled up a stool, and managed to get up to the sink. He picked up a dirty glass lying in the sink, filled it with lukewarm water, and brought it out to his dad. Dr. Coleman commented, "The glass may have been dirty and the water warm, but it was brought to me in perfect love." That is the essence of sanctification. We are each endowed with a self-forgetful heart—a heart that has been reoriented toward love.

EIGHT

Holiness as the Church Bearing Fruit

There are few more established routines in life than the traditional bedtime story. When our children were small, it was the only way a day could be brought properly to an end. The number of stories that we read, remembered from our own childhood or, quite frankly, made up on the spot during that sacred nightly ritual, must number in the thousands. It was Eugene Peterson who probably best captured the childhood request that every parent has heard so many times as they tuck their children into bed for the night: "Daddy, please tell me a story, and put me in it." Storytelling is one of the most basic human activities. All of our memories are built around stories. When we get together with our friends, what do we do? We tell stories. We exchange little narratives with each other. We laugh and we tell more stories. Life is not just filled with facts and information; it is an unfolding story. In the same way, the Bible is a grand narrative. God is unfolding a story, and as the ultimate Storyteller, He is putting us in it!

The Bible is the faithful record of that grand story. It continually calls us back to the story when we are all too often prepared to accept lesser stories and smaller narratives. God started writing us into His grand story when He created us in His own image and breathed into us the breath of life. (We explored this in chapter 2.) After the fall, as the story continued to unfold, we saw that the great theme of reestablishing God's presence is what makes us the people of God. This story is about more than keeping the Law, or getting circumcised. Those are all crucial marks of identity, but fundamentally it is about God's presence. Moses would later make this clear when he said to the Lord, "If your Presence does not go with us, do not send us from here. How will anyone know that you are pleased with me and with your people unless you go with us? What else will distinguish me and your people from all the other people on the face of the earth?" (Ex. 33:15–16). The consequence of sin at the fall recorded in Genesis 3 is death, which is, at its root, the loss of God's presence. The human race lives in perpetual exile from the Presence. Presence lost—presence regained—that's one of the main themes of this epic story! As noted in the last chapter, sin is more than the deeds we commit, or the breaking of God's law. Sin is fundamentally relational. Sin is all the places where we elect the absence of God in our lives. Holiness, therefore, is fundamentally about the presence of God being restored into our lives, our other relationships and, indeed, in the world.

As we continue reading the Old Testament, we read more about the unfolding of the grand story. Sometimes things happen that seem rather odd to us. Strange things are done; agreements are made with certain marginal people; promises are given; strange rituals are performed. There is a particularly long part of the story, which seems to go on endlessly, about curtains and a lot of special garments, and special pieces of furniture, like lampstands, and bowls, and a table, and a very fancy golden box with fierce-looking creatures on the lid, all crafted by these two guys named Bezalel and Oholiab. But like a ten-thousand-piece puzzle, slowly the pieces to the big story start getting placed on the table, and we begin to notice a few things. Like the time God said that this big tent—a mobile temple—they were constructing was called *mishkan*; the English renders this "tent of meeting" or "tabernacle," but the word is richer than that. It means "dwelling place." We finally begin to see the reason for all of these elaborate rituals and curtains and outer and inner rooms and a most holy place where the ark of the covenant was to be kept. All of this was about God reestablishing His presence. It was about holiness. In Exodus 25:8 God declared, "Have them make a sanctuary [*mishkan*] for me, and I will dwell among them." It's about the restoration of presence!

The same pattern was repeated years later when the people settled into the Promised Land, and under Solomon, the temple was constructed according to a precise pattern. Finally, in 1 Kings 8 we read the account of the ark of the covenant being brought into the temple and into the Holy of Holies. Picture the ark being brought in on long poles by the sons of Aaron. So many sheep and cattle were being sacrificed that they were unable to be counted. The priests brought the ark into the Holy of Holies and placed it beneath the wings of the cherubim. The priests could not even stand and minister because the presence of God was so powerful and manifest. Solomon declares in 1 Kings 8:13 that the temple will be a place for the Lord to dwell forever!

The Holy of Holies remained God's outpost in a sinful world that only knew of the absence of God. But in the fullness of time, the Grand Storyteller made a surprise move. He entered into the very history of His own making. God came in human flesh. We call this the *incarnation*. It is the ultimate invasion of the presence of God into the world. God's presence now dwells in His people, the church. "I will build my church," declared Jesus (Matt. 16:18). The church is destined by God to be the outpost of His holiness in the world. The original Holy of Holies was in a fixed location in the inner part of the temple in Jerusalem. At the crucifixion of Christ, the curtain that separated the Holy of Holies from the rest of the temple was torn in two from top to bottom (Mark 15:38). The new Holy of Holies now resides in the church of Jesus Christ. This means that there should be hundreds of thousands of Holy of Holies wherever God's people gather for worship! This is made possible because God's presence is now located in the gathered people of God. Jesus said, "For where two or three gather in my name, there am I with them" (Matt. 18:20). If the church ceases to be holy, then it amounts to the loss of the manifest presence of Jesus in the world.

Today, many have a broken, fragmented view of the church. We think of salvation as merely a personal transaction between ourselves and Jesus. But in God's design, the church is about much more. The church is not just the aggregate gathering of all the justified individuals who happen to come together. The church is what God is building in the world. It is the new Holy of Holies. Jesus Christ is the foundation, and He is building His church. You cannot fully enter into personal holiness unless and until you are rightly related to the church, the people of God. It is the church that is the lens through which we capture the glorious work of God and experience the manifest presence of God. The church of Jesus Christ is God's plan to manifest His presence and to demonstrate the fruit of His holiness in the world. Holiness, as we have seen, is not merely about eradicating sin in our lives. It is about the full manifestation of all the fruit of the Spirit through the church of Jesus Christ. We are preparing for that day in the New Creation when we will once again see the cosmic river with not one, but *two* trees of life, one on each side, bearing fruit. In the New Creation the gates are never closed. Open gates mean that we are no longer living in fear. Holiness must become embodied both personally and corporately in the life and witness of the church. This is why Jesus said, "For where two or three gather in my name, there am I with them" (Matt. 18:20). It is in the community of God's Spirit-filled people that the presence of Jesus is fully made manifest in the world.

NINE

Holiness and God's Mission in the World

When was the last time you read the prophecy of Joel? He lived in really difficult days when Israel was going into exile. Joel was calling *everyone* to repentance. I did a survey of Joel and found the following people he was calling to repentance: old people, young people, men, women, children, drunkards, farmers, servants, priests, Jews, non-Jews, the nation under covenant, nations not under covenant . . . He captured the whole human race. Like a voice crying out in the wilderness, Joel was telling the human race, "Stop! You're all going the wrong way!" Yet, in the midst of all this faithlessness and rebellion against God, Joel had a vision. At the very time when foreign armies were invading and capturing the people of God and taking them into exile, Joel had a vision of the last days: "And afterward, I will pour out my Spirit on all people. Your sons and daughters will prophesy, your old men will dream dreams, your young men will see visions. Even on my servants, both men and women, I will pour out my Spirit in those days" (2:28–29). Joel was living in the worst possible situation, yet he had a vision of the day when the Spirit would be poured out.

We see a similar theme in Jeremiah, who prophesied on the brink of and into exile. Nebuchadnezzar and his Babylonian hoards had repeatedly attacked Jerusalem, humiliating Israel. Jeremiah witnessed the final decades that dismantled the entire nation. Jews were being locked into chains and put on carts and taken to Babylon. Others were fleeing to Egypt, in disobedience to God, thinking they might be safe there. Toward the end of all this national humiliation, when the last exiles were being put in chains, Jeremiah did something that really seems crazy. He bought a piece of land. Isn't that amazing? Jeremiah 32:9 records that at the time of the exile, "I bought the field at Anathoth from my cousin Hanamel and weighed out for him seventeen shekels of silver." He went on to prophesy in verse 15: "This is what the LORD Almighty, the God of Israel, says: 'Houses, fields and vineyards will again be bought in this land.'" Jeremiah bought the field of Anathoth because he was caught up in a greater narrative. He was tuned into a narrative that was even louder than the deafening march of Babylonian armies. He could see beyond the Babylonian invasion to the final victory of God for the people of God! Jeremiah, like Joel, lifted up the eyes of his heart and he spoke the vision: "This is the covenant I will make with the people of Israel . . . I will put my law in their minds and write it on their hearts. I will be their God, and they will be my people. No longer will they teach their neighbor, or say to one another, 'Know the LORD,' because they will all know me, from the least of them to the greatest" (Jer. 31:33–34). The great weeping prophet is, it turns out, also a prophet of hope. He captured a glimpse of a better day.

We see this theme again at the beginning of the New Testament with John the Baptist, who stands at the end of a lot of promises, many of them unfulfilled. John declared, "I baptize with water. But one who is more powerful than I will come, the strap of whose sandals I am not worthy to untie. He will baptize you with the Holy Spirit and fire" (Luke 3:16). What is the theme that ties together such figures as Joel, Jeremiah, and John the Baptist? They are all pointing to a time when the future realities of God's rule and reign will break into the present world. These promises were not finally realized until the death, resurrection, and ascension of Christ and the coming of the Holy Spirit. These prophets were envisioning the full work of the triune God in the world. The full redemption of the world is not the work of the Son alone, but is, in fact, the work of the triune God. The Father plans the mission, initiates it, and is the great sending agent from patriarchs to prophets to His only Son. Jesus, the Son of God, is the full embodiment of the New Creation. He fulfills the Law, the priesthood, the sacrificial system, and the Suffering Servant. As the second Adam, on the cross and in His resurrection, He provides the final sacrifice and atonement, defeating the power of sin and death. The Holy Spirit is the empowering presence of God who applies all of the future realities of the New Creation into the gathered communities of the church.

Through the coming of the Holy Spirit, the holiness of God will not merely be written on tablets of stone like the Ten Commandments, but will be written on our very hearts. Once the holiness of God is written on our hearts, it is no longer static, as it is when it is on tablets of stone kept in the temple in the Holy of Holies. Now, the holiness of God is gloriously unleashed into the world. It becomes virally mobile.

Missional Holiness

This is what I call *missional holiness*. It is a holiness that extends to the ends of the earth, encompassing all peoples and nations. This is what finally moves us out from the long night of self-imposed exile and into God's full purposes in the world. The witness of the Spirit that begins by confirming faith in our personal lives becomes the power of the Spirit to produce fruit and to transform the world. We are called to spread scriptural holiness through the world. This is missional holiness: the Holy Spirit empowering believers for witness, service, evangelism, and church planting.

This viral, mobile holiness is crucial to a proper understanding of holiness, which not only embraces the full purging of sin within, but also sees the implications of holiness as both personal and corporate, both individual and systemic. Mobile holiness declares freedom for those who are enslaved by human trafficking in Bangkok. It announces the good news to the remaining unreached people groups in India, the countries of Indonesia and Iraq, and wherever people have not heard the good news of Jesus Christ. Mobile holiness shines the light of justice on child labor in China and establishes peace in broken homes in America. It sets the drug addicts free in our inner cities. You see, mobile holiness is viral, and there is no part of creation that is not declared to be under the lordship of Jesus Christ! As Christians we can never be content with merely a privatized faith that keeps the good news to ourselves. Rather, we claim the whole field. We look at the most dismal situation on the planet and we declare, in faith, that we will buy that field! We will buy the field of Anathoth even as the Babylonians are moving in! We'll buy the field of hope even when drugs still hold reign. We'll buy the field of faith even while Muslims remain resistant! We'll buy the field of reconciliation even when the divorce papers are on the table! Because in all of life we cannot help but hear the glorious strains of the New Creation! We have been caught up in a greater narrative!

A Wesleyan vision of holiness does not fall into the trap of overoptimism, which fails to take seriously the full force of both personal and corporate rebellion against God. However, it also avoids the trap of overpessimism, which can only rehearse the bad news and cannot see the New Creation already breaking into the world in the faith, life, experience, and witness of the church of Jesus Christ. We have a vision for the power of transforming righteousness in the world.

And the best part of all is that we're going to have a great time doing it! Who needs wine when we've got the Holy Spirit! We've kept the dour face too long. We live in the light of the Resurrection. We are the people of the risen Lord! Brothers and sisters, to be holy means to be filled with the Holy Spirit. Allow the Holy Spirit to break the chains of your despair! Allow Him to enable you to recapture a vision for His Grand Story.

TEN

Concluding Thoughts on Holiness

These meditations have not been the normal exposition on holiness. Rather, this has been an attempt to restore the larger framework through which holiness is made possible and by which the final purpose of holiness in the world is understood.

Holiness in the Contemporary World

We began by seeking to understand how all the attributes of God are united in the triune God. We pointed out a number of theological problems in the church today that impede the manifestation of holiness in the church. We have to restore the whole foundation of God's nature: His role as Creator, the purpose of redemption, the integral nature of His attributes, and so forth, just to have a proper conversation about holiness. The lack of catechesis in the church has left an

religious instruction

entire generation of Christians unsure about what it really means to embody a distinctive Christian identity. Our lives are often not dramatically different from the world. There are countless examples in the contemporary church where we are actually embracing the sins of the world and trying to sanctify them in the church, rather than living out the full realities of what it means to be God's chosen, peculiar people.

Holiness the Work of the Triune God

It has also become clear that we must reclaim the basic theological point that salvation is grander and more extensive than we have recognized. Salvation is the work of the triune God. We need to be justified through the work of Jesus Christ and be sanctified through the work of the Holy Spirit, all according to the purposes and for the glory of God the Father. You need to be certain that you have experienced a spiritual rebirth and the regenerating work of the Holy Spirit. You also need a distinct work of sanctification in your life. Sanctification is what reorients your heart away from sin and toward God. Entire sanctification is a doctrine that has become almost unknown among many of the "people called Methodist." John Wesley once wrote in a letter to Mrs. Crosby in 1761 that he had "six in one class [who had] received remission of sins and five in one band [who had] received a second blessing." Such a comment would be hard to find in today's Methodist catechism classes.

The Fruitfulness of Holiness

We have also learned that holiness is deeper than merely the eradication of sin in our lives. That is only half the work of God. Sanctification is not just about what we avoid, but what we produce: namely, fruitfulness. In Wesley's teaching, faith and fruit meet and are joyfully wed. The church has been passing on a truncated view of holiness that is forensic, private, negative, and static. Such a view has turned holiness into a legalistic, self-focused orientation, identified by what we "don't do." With that emphasis, holiness loses its missional power. We have sought to demonstrate that a fully restored doctrine of holiness focuses on the full range of holiness that is a very powerful, positive vision. It is relational because we are fully connected to one another in the church as well as to the triune God. Holiness is never less than personal holiness, but it is also fully corporate since it calls us into the church and embeds us in community. Holiness is a positive vision of the full in-breaking of the New Creation. It is not static, but virally mobile, bringing and bearing the presence of God to the ends of the earth.

Holiness for the World

Finally, these reflections on holiness reveal one of the great truths about how Methodists do theology. We are not so much interested in speculative points that can bring us into endless debates and discussions that distract us from the mission of God in the world. We are, at heart, a missional movement. Holiness must overflow to the ends of the earth. We remain fixed on the importance of helping men and women from every corner of the earth, to use Wesley's phrase, "to flee from the wrath to come." (*John Wesley*, Albert C. Outler, ed. (Oxford University Press, 1964), 178). In other words, we are a movement about salvation, in the full sense of that word; not merely justification, but the whole gift of salvation from justification to sanctification to final glorification when we will become like Christ.

We will live eternally because we have finally and fully been brought into vibrant relationship with the triune God, who embodies eternality in all its perfection. This is why some of our greatest theology is not found in hefty books (though we have written plenty of those!) but in hymns of worship. Powerful theology always erupts into praise and worship. Therefore, as in my previous devotional books, I asked my wife to write a hymn. This hymn is dedicated to the call to holiness and can be sung to the tune of "Beecher" (often used as the tune for Charles Wesley's great hymn "Love Divine, All Loves Excelling"), or to "Ode to Joy" (familiar to us as the tune of Henry van Dyke's great hymn "Joyful, Joyful, We Adore Thee," which derived from the wonderful tune penned by Beethoven in his final symphony). May this act of worship be our prayer to God to make us holy, even as He is holy.

Make Us Holy

(1 Peter 1:3–2:3)

You are holy—make us holy! Let our lives reflect Your name;
By Your Spirit's pow'r within us, be a sanctifying flame.
Not the work of human striving, but a change from deep
    within:
Redirect our core affections; free us from the bonds of sin.

You are holy—so our holy lives a shining light must be,
Purged from empty selfish living, filled with love that comes
    from Thee.
Born again of seed eternal, through the living Word of God;
Growing up in our salvation, tasting that the Lord is good!

You are holy, and You call us to be pure in all we do;
As your character is holy, so we would be holy, too.
Purified by true obedience, loving others from the heart;
Serving in the world with power which your Spirit does
    impart.

Call To Holiness

You are holy—may Your church embody perfect holiness;
May the love of Christ compel us to bring forth true
    righteousness.
Let the strains of New Creation echo through Your church
    today;
Sounding forth the consummation of that glorious Holy
    Day!

—Julie Tennent